LITTLE
IRISH
SONGBOOK

ILLUSTRATED BY
IAN McCULLOUGH

Chronicle Books

First published in 1992 by
The Appletree Press Ltd,
7 James St South,
Belfast BT2 8DL.
Illustrations copyright © Ian McCullough, 1992.
Typeset by Seton Music Graphics Ltd,
Bantry, Co. Cork. Printed in the UK.

First published in the United States in 1992
by Chronicle Books,
275 Fifth Street,
San Francisco, CA 94103

ISBN 0-8118-0187-X

9 8 7 6 5 4 3 2 1

Contents

Danny Boy 4

The Lark in the Morning 6

The Curragh of Kildare 8

The Galway Races 10

Believe Me, If All Those
  Endearing Young Charms 12

The Shores of Amerikay 14

The Black Velvet Band 16

Carrickfergus 18

I'm A Rover 20

Slieve Gallion Braes 22

Whiskey in the Jar 24

The West's Awake 26

The Bard of Armagh 28

My Singing Bird 30

Follow Me Up To Carlow 32

Clare's Dragoons 34

Pretty Susan, the Pride of
  Kildare 36

The Little Beggarman 38

The Wild Rover 40

The Jolly Beggar 42

I Will Walk With My Love 44

The Last Rose of Summer 46

The Jug of Punch 48

The Parting Glass 50

As I Roved Out 52

The Holy Ground 55

The Kerry Dances 58

Danny Boy

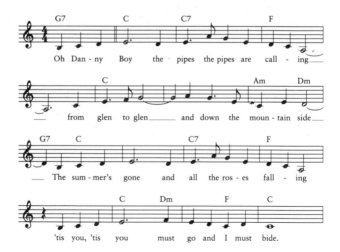

Oh Dan - ny Boy the pipes the pipes are call - ing

from glen to glen and down the moun - tain side

The sum - mer's gone and all the ros - es fall - ing

'tis you, 'tis you must go and I must bide.

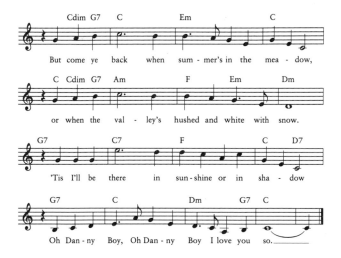

But come ye back when sum-mer's in the mea - dow,

or when the val - ley's hushed and white with snow.

'Tis I'll be there in sun - shine or in sha - dow

Oh Dan - ny Boy, Oh Dan - ny Boy I love you so.

And when ye come and all the flowers are dying,
If I am dead, as dead I well may be,
You'll come and find the place where I am lying,
And kneel and say an Ave there for me.
And I shall hear tho' soft you tread above me,
And all my grave will warmer, sweeter be
If you will bend and tell me that you love me,
Then I shall sleep in peace until you come to me.

The Lark in the Morning

Chorus: The lark in the mor - ning she ri - ses from her nest___ She goes

off___ ev - ery mor - ning___ with the dew all on___ her breast.___ And

like the jol - ly plough boy she whist - les and she sings___ She goes

home___ ev - ery ev - en - ing with the dew all on her wings.___

Oh, Roger the ploughboy, he is a dashing blade,
He goes whistling and singing over yonder green glade,
He met with pretty Susan, she's handsome I declare,
She is far more enticing than the birds in the air.

Chorus

One evening coming home from the rakes of the town,
The meadows being all green and the grass it being cut down,
If I should chance to tumble all in the new mown hay,
Oh, it's kiss me now or never, love, this bonny lass did say.

Chorus

When twenty long weeks they were over and were past,
Her mammy chanced to notice she'd thickened round the waist,
It was the handsome ploughboy the maiden she did say,
For he caused me for to tumble all in the new-mown hay.

Chorus

Here's a health to young ploughboys, wherever you may be,
That likes to have a bonny lass a-sitting on his knee
With a jug of good strong porter, you'll whistle and you'll sing,
For a ploughboy is as happy as a prince or a king.

Chorus

The Curragh of Kildare

The win-ter it is past and the sum-mer's come at last. The birds they are sing-ing in the trees. Their lit-tle hearts are glad, but straight I will re-pair to the mine is ver-y sad For my true love is Cur-ragh of Kil-dare For it's there I'll find

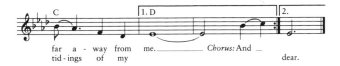

far a - way from me._____ *Chorus:* And __
tid - ings of my   dear.

The rose upon the briar by the water running clear
Brings joy to the linnet and the deer.
Their little hearts are blessed, but mine knows no rest
For my true love is absent from me.

Chorus

A livery I'll wear and I'll comb back my hair
And in velvet so green I will appear
And straight I will repair to the Curragh of Kildare
For it's there I'll find tidings of my dear.

O you that are in love, and cannot it remove
I pity the pain you do endure,
For experience lets me know that your hearts are full of woe
A woe that no mortal can cure.

Chorus

The Galway Races

As I rode down to Gal - way town to seek for re - cre -
There were pas - sen - gers from Lim - er - ick and more from Tipp - er -

a - tion on the sev - en - teenth of Au - gust me
ar - y, Boys from Con - nem - ar - a and a

mind being el - e - va - ted. There were mul - ti - tudes as -
flair of mar - ried la - dies, peo - ple from Cork ci - ty

sem - bled with their tick - ets at the sta - tion.____ Me
who were loy - al true____ and faith - ful ____ Brought

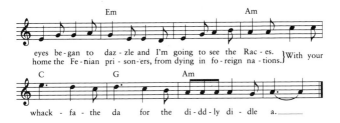

eyes be-gan to daz-zle and I'm going to see the Rac-es.
home the Fe-nian pri-son-ers, from dying in fo-reign na-tions. With your

whack - fa - the da for the di - dd - ly di - dle a.___

It's there you'll see the pipers and the fiddlers competing,
The nimble-footed dancers, a-tripping over the daisies.
There were others crying, cigars and likes, and bills for all the races,
With the colours of the jockeys and the price and horses' ages.
With your whack-fa-the-da, for the diddly-diddle-day.

It's there you'll see the jockeys, and they're mounted out so stately,
The pink, the blue, the orange and green, the emblem of our Nation.
When the bell was rung for starting, all the horses seemed impatient,
I thought they never stood on ground, their speed was so amazing.
With your whack-fa-the-da, for the diddly-diddle-day.

There was half a million people there, from all denominations,
The Catholic, the Protestant, the Jew and Presbyterian.
There was yet no animosity, no matter what persuasion,
But sportsman hospitality and induce fresh acquaintance.
With your whack-fa-the-da, for the diddly-diddle-day.

Believe Me, If All Those Endearing Young Charms

Be - lieve me, if all those en - dear - ing young charms which I

gaze on so fond - ly to - day___ Were to change by to - mor - row, and

fleet in my arms, Like___ fai - ry gifts fad - ing a - way.___ Thou would'st

still be a - dor'd, as this mo - ment thou art, Let thy

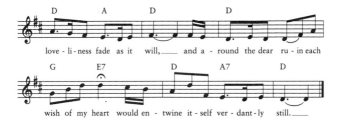

love - li - ness fade as it will,＿ and a - round the dear ru - in each
wish of my heart would en - twine it - self ver - dant - ly still.＿

It is not while beauty and youth are thine own,
And thy cheeks unprofan'd by a tear,
That the fervour and faith of a soul can be known,
To which time will but make thee more dear.
No, the heart that has truly lov'd, never forgets,
But as truly loves on to the close,
As the sunflower turns on her god, when he sets,
The same look which she turn'd when he rose.

The Shores of Amerikay

I'm bid-ding____ fa-re-well to the land of my

youth and the home I love so well._____ And the

moun-tains so grand round my own na-tive land, I'm

bid-ding____ them a-ll fare-well._____ With an

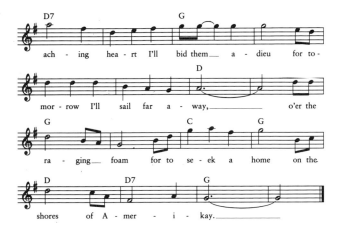

ach - ing hea - rt I'll bid them a - dieu for to-mor - row I'll sail far a - way, o'er the ra - ging foam for to se - ek a home on the shores of A - mer - i - kay.

It's not for the want of employment I'm going,
It's not for the love of fame,
That fortune bright, may shine over me
And give me a glorious name.
It's not for the want of employment I'm going
O'er the weary and stormy sea,
But to seek a home for my own true love,
On the shores of Amerikay.

And when I am bidding my last farewell
The tears like rain will blind,
To think of my friends in my own native land,
And the home I'm leaving behind.
But if I'm to die in a foreign land
And be buried so far far away
No fond mother's tears will be shed o'er my grave,
On the shores of Amerikay.

The Black Velvet Band

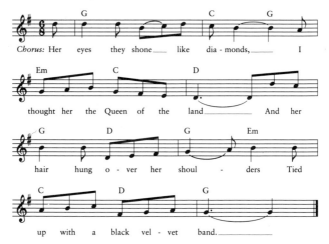

Chorus: Her eyes they shone___ like dia - monds,___ I thought her the Queen of the land___ And her hair hung o - ver her shoul - ders Tied up with a black vel - vet band.___

As I went walking down Broadway,
Not intending to stay very long,
I met with a frolicsome damsel,
As she came a-tripping along.
She was both fair and handsome,
Her neck it was white as a swan,
And her hair hung over her shoulder,
Tied up with a black velvet band.

Chorus

I took a stroll with this pretty fair maid
When a gentleman passed us by,
I knew she had the taking of him
By the look in her roguish black eye.
A gold watch she took from his pocket
And put it right into my hand
On the very first day that I met her,
Bad luck to the black velvet band.

Chorus

Before judge and jury next morning
Both of us had to appear
The judge he said to me, 'Young man,
Your case is proven clear.'
Seven long years' transportation,
Right on down to Van Dieman's Land
Far away from my friends and relations
Betrayed by the black velvet band.

Chorus

Carrickfergus

I wish I was _____ in Car - rick - fer - gus _____

_____ On - ly for nights _____ in Ball - y - gran

_____ I would swim o - ver _____ the deep - est o - cean

_____ on - ly for nights _____ in Ball - y - gran _____

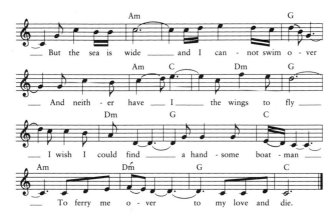

But the sea is wide _____ and I can not swim o - ver

And neith - er have I _____ the wings to fly _____

I wish I could find _____ a hand - some boat - man

To ferry me o - ver _____ to my love and die.

My boyhood days bring back sad reflections
Of happy hours I spent so long ago,
Of boyhood friends and my own relations
Are all passed on now, like drifting snow;
But I'll spend my days an endless rover,
Soft is the grass I walk, my bed is free;
Ah, to be back in Carrickfergus
On that long road, down to the sea.

But in Kilkenny it is reported
There are marble stones there, as black as ink,
With gold and silver I would support her
But I'll sing no more now till I get a drink.
I'm drunk today and I'm seldom sober,
A handsome rover from town to town,
Ah, but I'm sick now and my days are numbered
So come all you young men and lay me down.

I'm A Rover

I'm a ro - ver, sel - dom so - ber, I'm a
ro - ver of high de - gree It's when I'm
drink - ing I'm al - ways think - ing, How to
gain my love's com - pa - ny. I'm a - ny.

Though the night be as dark as dungeon,
Not a star to be seen above,
I will be guided without a stumble
Into the arms of my own true love.

He stepped up to her bedroom window;
Kneeling gently upon a stone
He rapped at her bedroom window:
'Darling dear, do you lie alone.

'It's only me your own true lover;
Open the door and let me in;
For I have come on a long journey,
And I'm near drenched unto the skin.'

She opened the door with the greatest pleasure,
She opened the door and she let him in;
They both took hands and embraced each other;
Until the morning they lay as one.

The cocks were crowing, the birds were singing,
The burns they ran free about the brae;
'Remember lass I'm a ploughman's laddie,
And the farmer I must obey.

'Now my love I must go and leave thee;
And though the hills they are high above,
I will climb them with greater pleasure,
Since I've been in your arms my love.'

Slieve Gallion Braes

Unaccompanied

As I went a - walk - ing___ one___ mor - ning in May, To view yon fair moun - tains and val - leys so gay, I was think - ing on those flow - ers, ___ all___

go - ing to — de - cay, That — bloom - a - round yon —

bon - ny, bon - ny, Slieve - Gal - lion Braes.

It's oft I did ramble with my dog and my gun,
I roamed through the glens for joy and for fun,
But those days are now all over and I can no longer stay,
So farewell unto ye, bonny, bonny Slieve Gallion braes.

How oft of an evening and the sun in the west,
I roved hand in hand with the one I loved best:
But the hopes of youth are vanished and now I'm far away,
So farewell unto ye, bonny, bonny Slieve Gallion braes.

O! it was not for the want of employment at home,
That caused the young sons of old Ireland to roam,
But the rents are getting higher and I can no longer stay,
So farewell unto ye, bonny, bonny Slieve Gallion braes.

Whiskey in the Jar

Capo 2nd

As I was go-ing o-ver the far famed Ker-ry moun-tains, I
He count-ed out his mon-ey, it made a pret-ty pen-ny, I

met with Cap-tain Far-rell and his mo-ney he was coun-ting I
put it in my pock-et and I gave it to my Jen-ny, She

first prod-uced my pis-tol and then put out my rap-ier Say-ing
sigh'd and she swore she ne-ver would be-tray me But the

stand and de-liv-er for you are the bold de-ceiv-er With my
devil take the wo-men for they nev-er can be ea-sy

Chorus:

24

whack fol the dol fol the da whack fol the dah di oh,

Whack fol the dah de oh There's whis-key in the jar.

I went unto my chamber all for to take a slumber,
I dreamt of gold and jewels and sure it was no wonder,
But Jenny drew my charges and she filled them up with water,
And she sent for Captain Farrell, to be ready for the slaughter.

Chorus

And 'twas early in the morning before I rose to travel,
Up comes a band of footmen and likewise Captain Farrell;
I then produced my pistol, for she stole away my rapier
But I couldn't shoot the water so a prisoner I was taken.

Chorus

And if anyone can aid me, 'tis my brother in the army,
If I could learn his station in Cork or in Killarney,
And if he'd come and join me we'd go roving in Kilkenny,
I'll engage he'd treat me fairer than my darling sporting Jenny.

Chorus

There's some take delight in the hurling and the bowling,
Others take delight in the carriages a-rolling;
But I take delight in the juice of the barley,
And courting pretty women when the sun is rising early.

Chorus

The West's Awake

When all be-side a vi-gil keep, The West's a-sleep, the

West's a-sleep. A-las, and well may E-rin weep that

Con-nacht lies in slum-ber deep, There lake and plain smile

fair and free, 'Mid rocks their guar-dian chiv-al-ry, Sing,

oh! let man learn li-ber-ty, from crash-ing wind and lash-ing sea!

That chainless wave and lovely land
Freedom and Nationhood demand
Be sure the great God never planned,
For slumb'ring slaves a home so grand,
And long a proud and haughty race
Honour'd and sentinell'd the place
Sing, oh! not e'en their sons' disgrace,
Can quite destroy their glory's trace.

For often in O'Connor's van
To triumph dashed each Connacht clan,
And fleet as deer the Normans ran
Through Curlieu's Pass and Ardrahan;
And later times saw deeds as brave,
And glory guards Clanricarde's grave;
Sing, oh! they died their land to save,
At Aughrim's slopes and Shannon's wave.

And if, when all a vigil keep,
The West's asleep, the West's asleep,
Alas! and well may Erin weep,
That Connacht lies in slumber deep;
But hark! a voice like thunder spake;
The West's awake! the West's awake!
Sing oh, hurrah! let England quake!
We'll watch till death for Erin's sake.

The Bard of Armagh

Oh list' to the lay of a poor Ir-ish har-per and

scorn not the string of his old with-ered hands, but re-

mem-ber those fin-gers they once could move shar-per to

raise up the strains of his dear nat-ive land.

It was long before the shamrock, dear isle's lovely emblem,
Was crushed in its beauty by the Saxon's lion paw;
And all the pretty colleens around me would gather,
Call me their bold Phelim Brady, the Bard of Armagh.

How I love to muse on the days of my boyhood,
Though four score and three years have fled by them;
It's king's sweet reflection that every young joy,
For the merry-hearted boys make the best of old men.

At a fair or a wake I would twist my shillelah,
And trip through a dance with my brogues tied with straw;
There all the pretty maidens around me gather,
Call me their bold Phelim Brady, the Bard of Armagh.

In truth I have wandered this wide world over,
Yet Ireland's my home and a dwelling for me;
And, oh, let the turf that my old bones shall cover,
Be cut from the land that is trod by the free.

And when Sergeant Death in his cold arms doth embrace,
And lull me to sleep with old Erin-go-bragh,
Be the side of my Kathleen, my dear pride, oh, place me,
Then forget Phelim Brady, the Bard of Armagh.

My Singing Bird

I have seen the lark so - ar high at morn to___

sing___ up___ in the blue, I have heard the black - bird___

pipe its song, the___ thrush___ and the lin - net

too. But___ none of them can sing so sweet, my

If I could lure my singing bird from its own cosy nest,
If I could lure my singing bird I would warm it on my breast
And on my heart my singing bird would sing itself to rest,
Ah—, would sing itself to rest.

Follow Me Up To Carlow

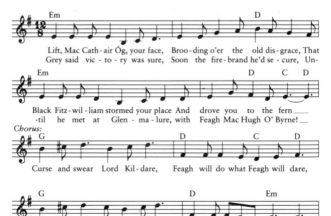

Lift, Mac Cath-air Óg, your face, Broo-ding o'er the old dis-grace, That
Grey said vic-to-ry was sure, Soon the fire-brand he'd se-cure, Un-

Black Fitz-wil-liam stormed your place And drove you to the fern___
-til he met at Glen-ma-lure, with Feagh Mac Hugh O' Byrne!___

Chorus:

Curse and swear Lord Kil-dare, Feagh will do what Feagh will dare,

Now Fitz-wil-liam have a care, Fal-len is___ your star low.

Up with hal-berd out with sword, On we'll go for by the Lord

Feagh Mac Hugh has giv-en the word, 'Fol-low me up to Car - low.'

See the swords of Glen Imail
Flashing o'er the English Pale,
See the children of the Gael
Beneath O'Byrne's banners.
Rooster of a fighting stock,
Would you let a Saxon cock
Crow out upon an Irish rock;
Fly up and teach him manners.

Chorus

From Tassagart to Clonmore
Flows a stream of Saxon gore,
Och! great was Ruari Óg O'More
At sending loons to Hades.
White is sick and Lane is fled–
Now for black Fitzwilliam's head–
We'll send it over dripping red
To Liza and her ladies.

Chorus

Clare's Dragoons

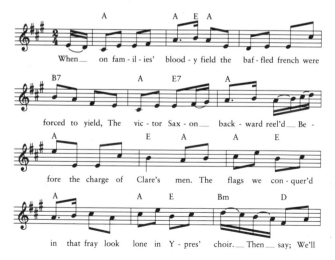

When on fam-il-ies' blood-y field the baf-fled french were

forced to yield, The vic-tor Sax-on back-ward reel'd Be-

fore the charge of Clare's men. The flags we con-quer'd

in that fray look lone in Y-pres' choir. Then say; We'll

win them com-pan-y to-day or brave-ly die like Clare's men. *Chorus:* Vi-ve là! For Ire-land's wrong, Vi-ve là! for Ire-land's right, And vi-ve là in bat-tle throng, for a Span-ish steed and sa-bre.

Another Clare is here to lead, the worthy son of such a breed,
The French expect some famous deed when Clare leads on his
  warriors.
Our Colonel comes from Brian's race, his wounds are in his breast
  and face,
The gap of danger's still his place, the foremost of his squadron.

Chorus

Oh, comrades, think how Ireland pines for exiled lords and rifled
  shrines,
Her dearest hope the ordered lines and bursting charge of Clare's
  men.
Then fling your green flag to the sky, be Ljmerick your battle cry,
And charge till blood floats fetlock high around the track of
  Clare's men.

Chorus

Pretty Susan, the Pride of Kildare

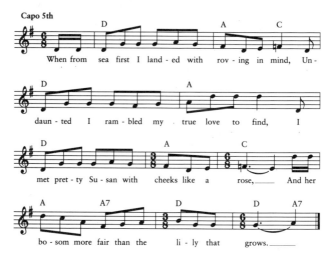

Capo 5th

When from sea first I land-ed with rov-ing in mind, Un-daun-ted I ram-bled my true love to find, I met pret-ty Su-san with cheeks like a rose, And her bo-som more fair than the li-ly that grows.

Her keen eyes did glitter like bright stars by night,
And the robes she was wearing were costly and white,
Her bare neck was shaded with her long raven hair,
And they call her pretty Susan, the pride of Kildare.

Sometimes I am jovial, sometimes I am sad,
Since my love she is courted by some other lad,
But since we're at a distance, no more I'll despair,
So my blessings on Susan, the pride of Kildare.

The Little Beggarman

Unaccompanied

I am a lit - tle beg - gar - man a beg - ging I have been Aye for three score and ten___ in this lit - tle isle of green And up___ to the Lif - fey___ down to Tess - a - gue And I'm known___ by the name___ of the Bold John - nie Dhu. Of

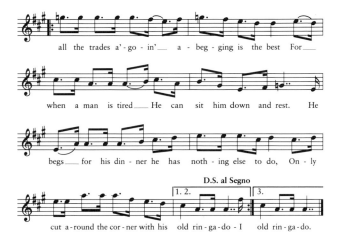

all the trades a'-go-in'___ a-beg-ging is the best For___

when a man is tired___ He can sit him down and rest. He

begs___ for his din-ner he has noth-ing else to do, On-ly

D.S. al Segno

1. 2.

3.

cut a-round the cor-ner with his old rin-ga-do-I old rin-ga-do.

I slept last night in a barn at Curraghbawn,
A wet night came on and I skipped through the door,
Holes in my shoes and my toes peeping through,
Singin' skiddy-me-re-doodlum, for old Johnny Dhu.

I must be gettin' home for it's gettin' late at night,
The fire's all raked and there isn't any light.
An' now you've heard me story of the ould ringadoo,
It's goodnight and God bless you from ould Johnny Dhu.

The Wild Rover

I've been a wild ro-ver for ma-ny's a year____

____ And I've spent all my mo-ney on whis-key and

beer____ And now I'm re-turn-ing with gold in great

store____ And I ne-ver will play the wild ro-ver no

night ___ We'll go no more a - rov - ing let the
moon ___ shine so bright ___ We'll go no more a - rov - ing.

He would not lie within the barn nor yet within the byer,
But he would in the corner lie, down by the kitchen fire,
And when the beggar's bed was made of good clean sheets
 and hay,
Down beside the kitchen fire the jolly beggar lay.

Chorus

The farmer's daughter she came down to bolt the kitchen door,
And there she saw the beggar standing naked on the floor.
He took the daughter in his arms and to the bed he ran
Kind sir, she says, be easy now, you'll waken our good man.

Chorus

Now you are no beggar, you are some gentleman,
For you have stole my maidenhead and I am quite undone.
I am no lord, I am no squire, of beggars I be one,
And beggars they be robbers all, so you are quite undone.

Chorus

She took the bed in both her hands and threw it at the wall,
Saying, go you with the beggarman, my maidenhead and all.
We'll go no more a roving, a roving in the night,
We'll go no more a roving, let the moon shine so bright,
We'll go no more a roving.

I Will Walk With My Love

I once loved a boy and a bold I - rish boy Who would

come and would go at my re - quest, And this

bold I - rish boy was my pride and my joy And I

built him a bower in my breast.

But this girl who has ta-ken my bon-ny, bon-ny boy Let her make of him all that she can, And whe-ther he loves me or loves me not, I will walk with my love now and then.

The Last Rose of Summer

'Tis the last rose of___ sum - mer Left___

bloo - ming___ a___ lone All her love - ly com___

pan - ions Are___ fa - ded___ and___ gone! No___

flow'r of___ her___ kin - dred, No___ rose - bud___ is___

nigh,_____ To re - flect back her_____

blu - shes, ˙Or____ give sigh____ for____ sigh.

I'll not leave thee, thou lone one,
To pine on the stem,
Since the lovely are sleeping,
Go, sleep thou with them;
Thus kindly I scatter,
Thy leaves o'er the bed
Where thy mates of the garden
Lie scentless and dead.

So soon may I follow,
When friendships decay,
And from Love's shining circle
The gems drop away!
When true hearts lie wither'd
And fond ones are flown,
Oh! who would inhabit
This bleak world alone?

The Jug of Punch

'Twas ver - y ear - ly in the month of June As

I was sit - ting in my room A small bird sang on an

i - vy bush And the song she sang was the Jug of Punch Too - ral

loo - ral lay Too - ral loo - ral lay Too - ral loo - ral lay Too - ral

loo - ral lay A small bird sang on an i - vy bush and the song she sang was the Jug of Punch.

What more diversion can a man desire,
Than to be seated by a snug coal fire,
Upon his knee a pretty wench,
And on the table a jug of punch.

Now when I am dead and in my grave,
No costly tombstone will I crave
Just lay me down in my native heath
With a jug of punch at my head and feet.

The Parting Glass

Oh,— all the mo - ney— e'er I had, I—

spent it in— good— com - pa - ny, And—

all the harm I've— e - ver done, a - las it was— to—

none but me, And all— I've— done for want— of— wit to

mem - 'ry now__ I__ can't re - call; So__ fill to me the__ par - ting glass, Good__ night and joy__ be__ with you all.

Oh, all the comrades e'er I had,
They're sorry for my going away,
And all the sweethearts e'er I had,
They'd wished me one more day to stay.
But since it falls unto my lot
That I should rise and you should not,
I gently rise and softly call,
Goodnight and joy be with you all.

If I had money enough to spend,
And leisure time to sit awhile,
There is a fair maid in this town,
That sorely has my heart beguiled,
Her rosy cheeks and ruby lips,
I own, she has my heart in thrall,
Then fill to me the parting glass,
Good night and joy be with you all.

As I Roved Out

Capo 5th

Am

As I roved out on a May mor - ning, On a

May morn - ning right ear - ly, I met my love a -

G **F** **G** **Am**

long the way, Oh__ Lord but she was ear - ly__

Chorus: **Am**

__ And she sang lilt a doo - dle lilt a doo - dle,

lilt a doo-dle dee and she hi-da-lan-da dee and she
hi-da-lan-da-dee and she lan - day.

Her boots were black and her stockings white,
And her buckles shone like silver,
And she had a dark and a rolling eye,
And her earrings tipped her shoulder.

Chorus

'What age are you, my nice sweet girl?
What age are you my honey?'
How modestly she answered me,
'I'll be sixteen age on Sunday.'

Chorus

I went to the house on the top of the hill
When the moon was shining clearly;
She arose to let me in,
For her mammy chanced to hear her.

Chorus

She caught her by the hair of the head,
And down to the room she brought her;
And with the root of a hazel twig,
She was the well-beat daughter.

Chorus

'Will you marry me now, my soldier lad?
Marry me now or never?
Will you marry me now, my soldier lad,
For you see I'm done forever?'

Chorus

'No, I won't marry you, my bonny wee girl,
I won't marry you, my honey,
For I have got a wife at home,
And how could I disown her?'

Chorus

A pint at night is my delight,
And a gallon in the morning;
The old women are my heartbreak,
But the young one is my darling.

Chorus

The Holy Ground

Capo 2nd

Fare - well my love - ly Di -

nah, A thou - sand times___ A - dieu_____ For we're

go - ing a - way from the Ho - ly Ground, And the

girls we all___ loved true_____ We'll___

sail   the   South___ Seas   o - ver   and___

we'll   re - turn   for   sure_____   To   see   a -

gain   the   girls   we   love   and the   Ho - ly

Ground___ once   more_____   To the   girl   I   do   a -

dore_____   And still   I   live   in   hope   to

see   the___ Ho - ly   Ground___ once   more._____

Oh, the night was dark and stormy,
You scarce could see the moon,
And our good old ship was tossed about,
And her rigging all was torn:
With her seams agape and leaky,
With her timbers dozed and old,
And still I live in hopes to see,
The Holy Ground once more.
You're the girl I do adore
And still I live in hopes to see,
The Holy Ground once more,
Fine girl you are!

And now the storm is over,
And we are safe on shore,
Let us drink a health to the Holy Ground
And the girls that we adore;
We will drink strong ale and porter
Till we make the tap room roar
And when our money is all spent
We will go to sea once more.
You're the girl I do adore
And still I live in hopes to see,
The Holy Ground once more,
Fine girl you are!

The Kerry Dances

O the days of the Ker - ry dan - cing, O the days of the

pip - er's tune, O for one of those hours of glad - ness,

gone a - las like our youth too soon. When the boys be -

gan to gath - er in the glen of a sum - mer night,

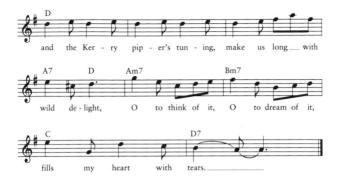

and the Ker - ry pip - er's tun - ing, make us long ___ with wild de - light, O to think of it, O to dream of it, fills my heart with tears. ___

Was there ever a sweeter colleen in the dance than Eily More,
Or a prouder lad than Thady as he boldly took the floor.
'Lads and lassies, to your places, up the middle and down again',
And the merry-hearted laughter ringing through the happy glen.
O to think of it, O to dream of it, fills my heart with tears.

O the days of the Kerry dancing, O the ring of the piper's tune,
O for one of those hours of gladness, gone alas like our youth
 too soon.